Hafsa Abdur- ewport, South Wales. She is half Alge ing predominately Irish. She is a poet who has about her mental health experiences as well as adding fiction to her poetry.

Her poetry ranges from subjects such as writing about her mental health, and identity. She has also written about reoccurring events about the pandemic and writes about what she is most passionate about.

I would like to dedicate this book to my family and friends and those who have guided me in the right direction.

Hafsa Abdur-Rahman

HAFSA'S POEMS

AUSTIN MACAULEY PUBLISHERS™
LONDON • CAMBRIDGE • NEW YORK • SHARJAH

Copyright © Hafsa Abdur-Rahman 2023

The right of Hafsa Abdur-Rahman to be identified as author of this work has been asserted by the author in accordance with sections 77 and 78 of the Copyright, Designs and Patents Act 1988.

All rights reserved. No part of this publication may be reproduced, stored in a retrieval system, or transmitted in any form or by any means, electronic, mechanical, photocopying, recording, or otherwise, without the prior permission of the publishers.

Any person who commits any unauthorised act in relation to this publication may be liable to criminal prosecution and civil claims for damages.

A CIP catalogue record for this title is available from the British Library.

ISBN 9781398481329 (Paperback)
ISBN 9781398483774 (ePub e-book)

www.austinmacauley.com

First Published 2023
Austin Macauley Publishers Ltd®
1 Canada Square
Canary Wharf
London
E14 5AA

I would first like to thank Austin Macauley Publications for wanting to work with me to publish my poetry.

I would also like to dedicate this book to my mother and father, who have helped me through my struggling times of my mental health over the years.

Secondly, I would like to thank my siblings, cousins as well as my nan and grandad and family in Algeria.

To finalise I would also like to thank my support worker/s and mental health nurses as well my doctor's past and present and Counsellors who have helped me.

To whom this may concern,
I have no writing experience, but I have been writing since Secondary School. Poetry has always been an interest to me, and I have found that poetry helps me to relax and enables me to unwind and express myself through writing. I wrote my first poem in 2012 and have been writing since.

Kind Regards,
Hafsa Abdur-Rahman

Poem 1
Surreal

Why are we stuck here?
All we do is cleanse and Bleach everything,
This continues and it's like history repeating itself, day by day,

When all I want to do is go to a beach and forget everything
Everyone thinks our world is surreal and if any of this is real?
Lots of despair as loved ones are gone and those in critical conditions, although it has coupled people together and saved those who were in dismay relationships.

When will this pandemic be over?
And those who are gone, will be cured from their suffering from this horrendous flu like virus, and will be remembered as the heroes in crisis,
There will come a day when Corona virus will be out of the way.

Poem 2
Ghosted

Why is it so empty?
Streets are ghosted
No one is about
It's the Corona, when will it end?
Queues are if the stars correlation connected
It feels so full
Yet it feels so empty
It has been over a month,
We are secluded in our houses
Allowed for only small distances and for daily walks,
We are stuck in a misery
Everyone eager to come out bustling with eager and frustration.
We want to hear will this end
but until then we wait.

Poem 3
Winter

Why is misty
Why is cold
All I can feel is frost and snow
This is the winter which we will always know
Can't it be summer?
we'll never know

Poem 4
All in the mind

Where am I?
I am so high and blue,
I begin to wonder will I ever go back
I begin to find it difficult to differ between vision and reality
and whether I will find a way out
Everything so abnormal and surreal
I begin to wonder why I am the only one who can see this,
Darkness and no way out, entrapped with my visions, their will come a day when light will enter, and all this will disappear.

Poem 5
Complete

The stars so bright you don't blind me
The sun so light it brightens me
Look up, look down, look all around
So blissful and merry you found me
So good so bad it dulls me, it's so sad

From sorrow to deceit to power that I want to greet
From upside down to a frown
Why does this world deceit?

From happy to sad through optimism which completes
From laughter to a cry the whole world frown
Frowns with disappointment and greed

Through bitterness and calmness, when will I realise when the world is complete?
Through nice and nasty which one makes sense or is just me who is not complete?

Poem 6
No Turning Back

You're so alone
You're so confused
You woke up and find your loved one gone
Just because of a war
Great memories destroyed
You begin to despair
You begin to think of the past and began to think of the future with regrets and no turning back,
The whole atmosphere begins to be surrounded with tears and sorrow
As they don't know what will happen tomorrow.

Poem 7
The Blazing war

You see me, I see you through hard and compassion
Through sorrow and happiness
These days I will always remember
Those melancholy days and the uplifting happiness through great love and compassion

Through blasting war and affectionate hugs, through smiles and frowns are never to be found.
Those frightful nights and sorrowful day, my heart, my heart will never be changed
Through hugs and love and blissful smiles, you will never see another child

All the days waiting through regret and anger, worried that it will never turn amber.

Stop
Stop
Stop stop!!!!!!!!!!!!!!!!!!!!!!!!!!!!!!!!!!!
The command will never stop

Poem 8
Lullaby

Sing me a lullaby
Your voice is so soft and sweet
Sing me a song
And your melody is complete
Draw me a picture because, I know it will be so neat
Write me a rhythmic poem and gather your thoughts, so we can speak
Hum me a rhythm so I can sleep

Poem 9
Without You

Without you
I am not complete
Without you
it's like losing a piece of a puzzle
Without you
I feel that there is no hope
Without
you I can't live
But with you is a completely different story

Poem 10
Puzzled Me

Your eyes sparkle like the sunshine
Your voice is as soft as a whisper
Your shadow follows each corner of my mind
And when I look for you
You seem to disappear
When I think about you and am without you
I feel empty, deep, and abandoned
But when I imagine you, the great smile widens and almost fills the atmosphere, and you create a great surrounding for me
When I see the moon, your reflection appears instead of it as these puzzles me as nothing is greater than the moon.
There will come a day when I see the great reflection of the moon but until we meet,
You will surround the objects like the sky, stars, and the sun.

Poem 11
Together Again

You make me smile
You make me laugh
You bring me great happiness
You bring me joy
I wept the day that we were not together
My darkest thoughts gathered whilst you weren't there
The day uplifts when the day comes for you to be near
Your speech is as soft as a whisper
You voice is melodic as a church choir
and we together harmonise together
Come back, my love
we will be together forever

Poem 12
Heartache

You broke my heart
Your words broken me into a million pieces
And now you are satisfied with yourself
It was as if you didn't have a dark side
however, you are much darker
There was a time when you were kind, considerate and cheerful
Until you let your anger take over
They do not see you how I do
But one day you will begin to unveil yourself and your true self will show.
One thing is certain I am the happiest I have ever been without you
However, I wish for your happiness even though you didn't wish me for mine.

Poem 13
One True Love

I love the way you talk
You make my smile
You make me feel, as if I need nobody
One half of you makes me complete
You bring me success and joy
My heart lingers only for you
Your needs satisfy me
You're my true love
Nothing will ever replace you
When I look at you
it's as if the stars align together
It's like the universe is uniting us together and we are destined for each other.

Poem 14
Il N'est Jamais Trop Tard

You were never connected to me
You drained me and my emotions
My heart was ripped out because of you
My tone harshened because of you being emotionless
You filled me with anger and regret
You made me lifeless and have no hope
Now I am the best and feel the best
Life doesn't end because I don't have you
Yolo, so enjoy life while it lasts
Il n'est jamais trop tard to live your best life
Love is the best it's also the worst
But once you have it,
It fills all the void within.

Poem 15
Longing to Be Yours

I believe you're the right one for me
My heart lingers for you
A day has gone without you
and you are greatly missed
A little bit dismayed as you're not present
Our minds both alike, however still different
Your husky voice still in my mind.
I like the way you talk about the future with great passion and emphasis,
There's never a dull moment with you and,
I wish for you to be mine.

Poem 16
My True love

I loathe you, although I once loved you
You have sucked the happiness from me
Me and you are no more
You can find happiness elsewhere without me
You have made me lose all hope for love
However
I am not giving up
I will find love without you and once I do
You will be forgotten for ever and ever
When will my true love come?
I am waiting for you from dawn to dusk
I search from universe to universe to find you
However, this is still a great challenge
I will soon be destined with my one true love
Until then I wait for my time to come.

Poem 17
Together Forever

You had a place in my heart
Now you have been replaced with another
Why did you have to disappoint me?
I thought we were to be together forever

Even though you have broken my heart
I am glad you have moved on
I don't despise you
even though you broke my heart
Not even a single message of why you decided to go your separate path,
What more can I say?
Even though greatly disappointed me and didn't say a single goodbye my way.

Farewell my love
you won't be greatly missed
A simple oxymoron for a sweet bitter twist,
Goodbye my old friend, I will look back and remember that dark foggy mist

You will be erased from my memory like a swipe button, and this will never be switched

Poem 18
The Oppressor

Families were reunited with an oppressor,
That will be £700 please,
Bash Bosh,
Melancholy days never ended,

1000 people waiting
Great anguish and sorrow
This day tomorrow
Ending in sorrow
Two boys crying
The oppressor never holding back
Families hurt
Though guilt
No Tranquillity
Like Shakespeare's play
Romeo with no Juliet

30 years later
No different
Same people
Same gossip

Fleeing to and from country to country,
20,000 husbands
40,000 wives
No fairness
No respect

Poem 19
The Obstacle

There once lived a man
Very brave, very courageous
Through hard obstacles and reoccurring challenges
34 girls, his strength grew and grew

One boy ill
hardship which kept reoccurring
Nurses, doctors
boy dismayed,
No accepting reality
Denial, Denial
Ones said

Boy and girl both living in a daydream
Witnessing of what would do
Struggles of hardship
and
It has felt as if it was the great depression,

Boy and girl felt hurt abandoned

No one to hear them out

Trapped!

Poem 20
The hardship between families

A wife dismayed
Through her betrayal
45 kids not knowing their dad

Each littered and picked amongst other places
Many adopted, no home, real struggle
Bonding between boy and girl
Horrible family
No bonding between the two
Families over feud
only reunited by destiny
A dreamer
A feeling
an instinct

Four leaders
No compassion,
20,000 on one side 6 dictators,
Children entrapped
psychic moments

Many lived each battling their deception
2 girls stop speaking, why have you done this?
Phone rings……………………
The episode starts again………………………………

Poem 21
Long Gone

There was once a boy
who was troubled?

He ran away
He was afraid
and no concept of accepting reality

Parents dismayed
Truly confused

This boy was infuriating, confused, angered and so many more emotions

Bullied

No sticking up for himself
another boy strong defended himself
courageous in many ways

Troublemakers
Teacher trying to figure things out

The boy's father horrid, dictator and possessive,
No one wanted the truth to unveil

Deception
Deception
Deception

Struggles from truth and reality

Your words of wisdom
Will come to me one day

Poem 22
Poverty

A family lived through poverty
Old furniture
Sat on floor
No beds
Two struggling parents
Working hard to provide for their children,

Individuals laughed,
Frowned and laughed at this family

No empathy,
No one understood

A brother helped although struggling through his finances,
Belittled by one another

Sisters
Brothers

All laughed

that's all I am going to say.

Poem 23
The Happy Life

Ones lived through one's melancholy
however pressured life
These unpopular leaders
Dictatorship and horrendous storms that one encounters in one's life

A beautiful necklace that sprinkled and shined
and that one could wish they were dined,
There are beautiful moments in life
where one is loved
however, happiness is gone

Cruel behaviour from all and of that of you
Guilt of losing such a beautiful memory
Funerals shouldn't have to reunite us

Weddings however should bring us happiness, content, and felicity,
Children frolicking through happiness and merriness,

You could wish
you could relive these moments
A celebration of one
when one is born,

Great rejoice and happiness to be rejoiced.

Poem 24
A Lovely Friend

A boy visited this family
He was a lovely boy
Helping her to show her strength
She was ignorant,
Too proud to show the family their mistakes
Too scared to comfort her fears
Courage, however, is the Absence of fear
A great philosopher once stated,

The lady was right
He tried
She tried
Nothing conquering her foolish ways
Blocked from the memory, memory shattered.

Poem 25
The Asylum

A boy once visited the asylum,
Horrified by the old ruins and
eerie memories created of the haunted hospital

A boy used to see an old lady
laying on the willow tree
Opium in their bloodstream, amongst other illusions,

Nurse help me
However
No help was ever received
Good Doc, amongst bad Nurses
Good Nurse, amongst bad Doc

These are the struggles in being in the Asylum

Poem 26
The loving family

A loving family brought a young boy to their house
Welcomed him
Fed him
and changed his melancholy state of mine

The couple were lovely
the boy's father was jealous and tried to ruin the relationship
for his family
You didn't do this
Boy horrified
wished he could apologise
Boy doesn't want no contact with family

A day will reunite us hopefully and these issues will be resolved

Poem 27
Previous Bestowed

I am glad you're gone
You weren't the right one for me
Great memories made however shattered by you
And only by you...................
The future will lead to something greater.

I will meet someone more
Caring
Kinder
Compassionate about our love
Never bitter like you

I fell blindly for your love
Although these mistakes are to be made
I rejoiced when no one else rejoiced for you
I had faith in you when you broke my heart

I still think about you
Think of what our future would have been like
however

We are destined for certain of things and
You were not meant to be
Goodbye my previous bestowed

Poem 28
What You Have Sent Me from Above

Your voice stuck in my head
Louder and louder, it gets each day
I pray for you to go
You play on my mind

I wish
I could hear you no more
Yet your voice remains within
Are you with me for a reason?
Only the lord above knows

You make me fret over such silly things
But push me to do what I love
Maybe you should stay by my side

However
I don't want your darkest deepest thoughts.

Poem 29
The One Above

I love how you guide me to do some positive things

However

It's a nightmare
when the darkest side appears
Please help cure me God
and cure me from me from this illness
which you have given me that from above

CPSIA information can be obtained
at www.ICGtesting.com
Printed in the USA
BVHW060909050323
659635BV00010B/441

9 781398 481329